Gifted To:

_____

Blessings From:

_____

FOREVER GRATEFUL
to
GOD

*Sacred Writings from the Lord
and Devotional Journal*

Kerry M. Hirsch

XULON PRESS

Xulon Press
2301 Lucien Way #415
Maitland, FL 32751
407.339.4217
www.xulonpress.com

Unless otherwise indicated, Scripture quotations taken from the King James Version (KJV) – *public domain.*

Paperback ISBN-13: 978-1-6628-2920-8
Ebook ISBN-13: 978-1-6628-2921-5

DEDICATION

I'd like to dedicate this book to my two Fathers, my Heavenly Father and my Father who left this earth too soon. Thank you for taking good care of him Lord and for healing his heart. Thank you for waking me up and never giving up on me! Thank you for the words that you put on my heart to share with others. I am so humbled and so very Grateful!

✝

"And whatsoever ye do in word or deed, do all in the name of the Lord Jesus, giving thanks to God and the Father by him."

Colossians 3:17

"The Lord hath appeared of old unto me, saying, Yea, I have loved thee with an everlasting love: therefore with lovingkindness have I drawn thee."

Jeremiah 31:3

INTRODUCTION

W hen you are in the eye of the storm it's hard to focus and recognize your gifts. The enemy is constantly causing distractions and feeding you lies to deceive you. It is during your storms where the opportunity to listen and lean on the Lord can become a Blessing. Trust in His timing and His plans for you. Let Him guide you to your Divine destinations. Being still and focusing on Him will keep you in a place of Peace and help Strengthen your Faith.

The time is now to share what the Lord has put on my heart. He'd wake me up in the wee hours of the night when the house was still and quiet. The pure reflection of what He needed me to be so I could hear His words flow into my heart. There were times when I would receive them in first person. I was completely caught off-guard when it happened, and any time after that. I didn't question Him and continued to transfer whatever He put in my heart onto paper. The 6 writings in first person are: *Move Forward in Faith, *The Path, *I Lift You up My Child, *Faith Brings Hope, *My Ways, and *A Forgiving Heart.

I'm still not sure why God chose a Sinner and Commoner like me. I struggled in school and didn't like reading books. I had trouble comprehending what I read because I was such a day-dreamer, and yet He gave me these words that have now turned into a book. God is So Amazing! I am Forever Grateful for this journey and those quiet evenings of listening and writing His words. I am also Grateful for my Family and all of their Love and support. I am Grateful for my Prayer Warriors who have listened to these Sacred Writings, and encouraged me with their steadfast prayers.

I sincerely Hope there is something on these pages that encourages you and gives you Peace. I've included a journaling section for your personal use as well. I Hope that your Prayer pages are one day filled with answered prayers that will help build your Faith on your journey with Jesus. I Hope the Gratitude pages help to give you a new perspective on your life and shift your focus back to the Lord's divine plans and His timing for you. When you come from Gratitude, your negativity falls to the wayside and your eyes see what your heart needs to soften and Appreciate all He provides for you. I Hope you make time for yourself to be still and listen to Him and the Sacred Writing pages get filled with many words and revelations that the Lord puts on your heart. I Hope the Visions and Dreams pages overflow with whatever He has been filling up your mind and heart with! Lastly, I Hope the Blessings and Miracles pages reflect the abundant Blessings and undeniable Miracles that you witness and receive. May they keep you Believing and Strengthening you to continue along your well-lit path.

We are here to listen to Him, Trust in Him, Glorify Him, and be a Blessing to others. We are not here to hide the gifts He has given us under a bed or a bush. I am truly humbled and Grateful to God, because as hard as the enemy tried to keep me down, God kept getting me up to write. May these Sacred Writings lift you up and lead you to write whatever He puts on your heart. Be Blessed today and always!

☦

"There is one body, and one Spirit, even as ye are called in one hope of your calling; One Lord, one faith, one baptism, One God and Father of all, who is above all, and through all, and in you all."

Ephesians 4:4-6

"Ye are of God, little children, and have overcome them: because greater is he that is in you, than he that is in the world."

1 John 4:4

TABLE OF CONTENTS

Part 1

THE DECISIONS YOU MAKE,
DETERMINE THE PATH YOU TAKE.

GRATITUDE

Start each day by Thanking your Heavenly Father first. Before you ask for anything, you must be Grateful for everything. Be Thankful for Him meeting you right where you're at, even if it's not where you want to be. Be Thankful for His Love, His Forgiveness, and for His Blessings both big and small. Be Thankful for His Courage to help you take another step, even when you think you can't. Be Thankful for all of your trials, for it is then that you learn to lean on Him and build your Faith. Every day is an opportunity to be Grateful for the abundant Blessings God provides you. Be Grateful for His Patience as He teaches you to forgive, let go, and yield to Him.

We tend to hold on tighter when our trials get tougher. His ways are not our ways. Instead of asking Him why, be Grateful that He is giving you the Strength to move forward and recognize what you need to see. Any opportunity to lean on Him is a Blessing, even though it may not seem like it at the time. It can be very difficult to be in a place of Gratitude when things aren't going as you had planned. While what is set before you may not seem ideal, the way you handle it may be the lesson at that time. Purge out what surfaces and doesn't serve your spirit anymore. As hard as it may be to endure, your Gratitude for whatever you are facing will give you the Courage to carry on.

Embracing Gratitude for all of your trials is an important part of your Faith. The picture in your mind may not match what you wanted to see along your path. Be Grateful for the journey to wherever He leads. If the scenery isn't changing then neither are you. He will continue to put you through the same trials and tribulations until you change. Having eyes to see and ears to hear His words of wisdom are a Blessing. All of your pride must be cast aside and then your willing heart will be Grateful for the lesson at hand. There are times you may ignore what is right in front of you, it could be as simple as having more compassion for others. Gratitude can turn even your darkest moments into something so compelling that when you Praise Him the Peace will be undeniable and overcome you. Your eyes will be opened, your ears ready to hear, and your Appreciation for the simplest of things may be all you needed to do to turn a situation around.

Stay in a place of Gratitude and Praise Him throughout your day! Be Grateful for all of your trials and triumphs, Divine Delays, Divine positioning, and Divine appointments. Be Grateful for any opportunity to lean on Him and build your Faith in Him! Be Grateful for the moments you are listening, learning, growing, reflecting, and releasing the burdens you don't need to carry. Be Grateful in knowing that He wants what is Best for You! Be Grateful that His Son died on the cross for you and your sins. Be Grateful that He is all you need and will carry you through your storms. He is always with you, and He will never leave you or forsake you. His unconditional Love for you is beyond what your mind can ever comprehend! Be Grateful that His Will, His Way, and His Timing is perfect in all things. Be Grateful that He is in control and always sitting on The Throne.

My Prayer

Thank You Father for this day! Thank You for Your Mercy and Your Grace. Thank You for Your Love and Forgiveness. Thank You for meeting me right where I'm at, and for never giving up on me. Thank You for Your Patience. Thank You for choosing me. Thank You for discernment and clarity, and showing me what I need to see. Thank You for helping me to be Patient and Obedient. Thank You for the opportunity to lean on You, and for the Strength to persevere through all of my storms. Thank You for never leaving me or forsaking me. Thank You for carrying me when I needed it most. Thank You for getting everything into Divine Order and for your Divine Timing in all things. Thank You for opening doors to walk through with ease and Grace. Thank You for closing the doors that need to be closed, and removing the people who need to be removed. Thank You for putting people on my path to give a word in season to, or to receive a word from. Thank You in advance for all of your Blessings both big and small! Thank You for providing all of my needs by your riches in glory!

I would like to pray for _____. I lift up _____ to You Lord. Please put an extra hedge of protection around _____. Please shower _____ with your undeniable Love and Peace. Please heal _____ heart and remove any unforgiveness or resentment that _____ is carrying. Please open _____ eyes to see Your path and _____ ears to hear Your voice. Please give _____ the Courage needed to walk by Faith and not by sight. Thank you in advance for giving _____ Hope to rely on Your Divine Timing. Thank You in advance for answering all of these prayers!

I Praise You, I Honor You, I Trust You, I Believe in You, and I Give You all the Glory Father! Amen!

✝

"Rejoice in the Lord always: and again I say, Rejoice. Let your moderation be known unto all men. The Lord is at hand. Be careful for nothing; but in every thing by prayer and supplication with thanksgiving let your requests be made known unto God. And the peace of God,

which passeth all understanding, shall keep your hearts and minds through Christ Jesus."

Philippians 4:4-7

"Know ye that the Lord He is God: it is He that hath made us, and not we ourselves; we are His people, and the sheep of His pasture. Enter into His gates with thanksgiving, and into His courts with praise: be thankful unto Him, and bless His name. For the Lord is good; His mercy is everlasting; and His truth endureth to all generations."

Psalms 100:3-5

GOD'S TIMING

T oday you are here, on this day, in this moment, this is where God has placed you, not misplaced you. Yield and listen to the Lord and relinquish your control and allow Him to take over your life! Let Him lead the way and help you with the lessons to learn from, and walk away from. Rely on His Ways and His Divine timing to eliminate the distractions and worldly thoughts that seem to overtake you.

The hardest part of your journey with Jesus can be surrendering and realizing you are not in control. Faith is letting go so you can Trust in His Timing without looking ahead and wondering how He will get everything into Divine order. Know what your limit is and know when to stop. His pace is filled with Grace and Blessings. Pushing yourself is a spirit driving you, yield your vessel and allow God to guide you. Procrastination can keep you stuck and in bondage. The energy used to think about accomplishing a task, can be the energy you use to complete the task. Pray on it, start on it, tackle it, and be done with it! When you finally invite God in to take over your timelines, you'll need to get out of His way and follow His timeframes with ease and Grace.

If plans change, it's Him. If someone is removed, it's Him. If you don't get what you want, when you want it, you're being reminded of who is still on The Throne, and it's Him!

While there will always be trials and tribulations, His daily plans for you are divinely timed. Let go of any sorrow and Trust that what lies ahead is what His plans are for you. When He thinks you are ready, He will show you what you need to see and guide you in a Divine direction.

Today and every day, He will be by your side, longing for you to Trust in His timelines. Wait on the Lord and listen to where He wants to guide you on your daily walk. Trust that He has everything in Divine Order and that His Timing is Perfect in all things!

✝

"This is the day which the Lord hath made; we will rejoice and be glad in it."

Psalm 118:24

"Jesus Christ the same yesterday, and today, and for ever."

Hebrews 13:8

BLESSINGS

The Blessings from the Lord come in many forms, and always at the right time. His timing is perfect in all things. Learning to put Him first, yielding to Him, and giving Him all the Glory will reap great rewards of Peace and Blessings.

Blessings can arrive when you least expect it. Once you realize that You are Worthy to receive the Blessings He has for you, it is then that you can move forward in Faith and Gratitude. Even when it seems you're out of prayers and exhausted all of your Hope to receive a Blessing, God will step in and Bless you in ways you've never dreamed of. Not all Blessings may seem like one at first; if a door closed that you had hoped to walk through, if someone was removed from your path, seeing a person for who they really are, or a situation for what it really is. None of these seem like God's favor, but His plans may be in learning discernment. He will give you eyes to see and ears to hear and He knows when you are ready to receive a Blessing. He will answer your prayers in His timing. You may receive a Blessing from someone you don't know and haven't been a part of your journey. God can use people in many ways to Bless you. He can put anyone on your path to deliver a word in season, or a smile that brings a ray of Hope. Remember to Bless others along your path knowing what it feels like to receive. Give and it shall be given unto you.

You never know what He has in store for you. You can waste precious time and energy trying to maneuver your way down a road you're not to be on, a detour from the path He has put you on. You get impatient and want the results you think you should have but what are you learning then, frustration not Faith. Essentially you are turning away from Him, His plans, and the path He has carefully mapped out for you. Your Faith may be decreasing along with your patience and you get discouraged and lose sight of Him. The enemy waits for these moments. You need to focus on The Lord and Trust the timing of His Blessings that He has for you. Recognize and be Thankful for the well-lit path that leads to your Blessings. He will bring forth many more if you are Grateful for the journey, yield to Him, and Trust in His Timing.

There are times when a Blessing may also be in learning humility. When you try to get what you want and get ahead of God, He will humble you and show you that He is still in charge and sitting on The Throne. Humility comes before honor. Blessings are different for everyone and are delivered when He thinks you need them most. Never lose Hope and speak life over everything believing that your Blessing is coming. The ability to recognize His Blessings and being Grateful for them whenever they arrive is what God wants from you. Being a Blessing to others and sharing His unconditional Love is a way to Glorify Him. Teach others to receive His Blessings and His Glory will touch their hearts and be magnified all over the globe. May you always be ready to receive His abundant Blessings wherever you are on your journey with Jesus.

"O taste and see that the Lord is good; blessed is the man
that trusteth in Him."

Psalm 34:8

"Blessed be the Lord God, God of Israel, who only doeth wondrous things. And blessed be His glorious name for ever: and let the whole earth be filled with His glory; A-men', and A-men'."

Psalms 72:18 & 19

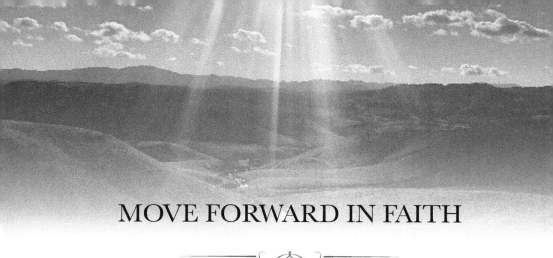

MOVE FORWARD IN FAITH

Y our Faith has sustained you and kept you moving forward. There are days when I know you didn't think you could continue but as you know, I carried you. Your Strength and access to My Word will keep you going. Let go of the thoughts that are not of Me, for they will keep you in the natural world and away from Me.

My Word is the best way to start your day. My Child it is the doing and the intention of your heart that sets it apart from a to-do list item. Know that I am your focus and set your goals. The distractions of the world will keep you stagnant, but I will set you free from all of it. Continue to make great strides forward in Faith. You must keep your Godly thoughts intact and your eyes fixed on Me as mine are on you. Keep your time constraints realistic and balance your rest, exercise, and your time alone with Me as part of your everyday routine.

Move forward in Faith and always come from a place of Love. Perfect Love casts out all fear. Yield to Me and do not react. You are not the Captain of the Ship anymore, lift up the anchor and look at the horizon, as far as the eye can see there are calm seas. The storm is over for now. Trust in Me to Bless your days to come. You have nothing to fear, you have Me to Trust, and a Peaceful horizon always in sight. Move forward in Faith by

Yielding to Me, standing on My Word, and Trusting that the rewards to come will be from persevering through your storms. Never lose your focus on Me or your Faith in Me. I am always by your side and will carry you if needed. I will light your path and guide your way in hopes that you will build your Trust in Me, so you can continue to move forward in Faith.

✝

But Jesus said to him, "No one, after putting his hand to the plow and looking back, is fit for the kingdom of God."
Luke 9:62

"I can do all things through Christ which strengtheneth me."
Philippians 4:13

HIS LIGHT

A ray of light can shine through the darkest storms and be seen differently by everyone. A ray of light can represent a ray of Hope and give you the Strength to carry on. Choosing to be guided by His light, following His lead and walking along His path is your choice; a good choice, and one that must be made without wavering. As you draw your Strength from Christ, your path will be well-lit by His Presence. His rays of Hope are what you need to cling to, knowing that the source is Him to help guide you along the way.

There are times when it seems you are headed to a familiar place of pain. He can gently help you uproot the sorrow, the guilt, the shame, the pride, or unforgiveness. You may have needed to revisit that old place in order to finally surrender and let it all go. The enemy doesn't want it brought to light, he'd rather keep you isolated and struggling with self-condemnation. It takes Courage to admit that you need prayers when there is something wrong. Once things are brought to light they can be seen for what they are and dealt with accordingly. Our sorrows and circumstances can become an idol and our focus always needs to fixate on Jesus. Out of the darkness comes power and freedom that break the chains and won't allow the enemy to keep you in bondage.

The Lord will find a way to get your attention and shift your focus on Him as He lights your way. He also wants you to fellowship with those you care about and lift them up allowing His light to shine through you. Open up your heart to being healed and filling the voids with His Love and light. The day will come when you recognize that all of it needed to be brought to light in order to be released and move forward in Faith. Your Obedience will always be rewarded, so Trust the journey to your Divine destination. He chastens those He Loves and prepares your willing heart to receive more of His unconditional Love.

Your life is His life. You are an example of Hope when you share His light that can be seen by others who are searching aimlessly in the darkness. Taking the next step of Faith can inspire others to do the same. Walk through your storm with the endurance and perseverance of a Warrior. The ray of light that you choose to see is always the brightest when you follow Him and His lead. For it is in your darkest hours that His light shines so bright. He is The Only Way, The Only Truth, The Only Light, and The Only Unconditional Love that you will ever need!

✝

"For thou art my lamp, O Lord: and the Lord will lighten my darkness."

2 Samuel 22:29

"Let your light so shine before men, that they may see your good works, and glorify your Father which is in heaven."

Matthew 5:16

THE PATH

The path is for your eyes to see, for the eyes of the beholder sees many different things. Some details may be overlooked but the memories are not forgotten. Your heart tries to deflect what it must to preserve it. The path may not be easy so discern what to take on and I will light the way and guide your heart and mind to see and hear My Truth. An open and willing heart, ready to receive My Love will be ready for the journey. Your Trust in Me will give you the Courage and perseverance you'll need to walk through the fiery trials and tribulations.

When the road seems barren and long I will place you on a path with new scenery. Take it all in, for the lessons on this road can take a different turn. Your lesson may be to understand that I am always here for you with open arms, and that I will carry you when you need Me to. The same scenario may come up again giving you the opportunity to respond differently and stand firmly in your Faith. Sometimes the path is paved with subtle distractions tempting you to go astray. Don't take the dark detours, instead stay on your well-lit path and never lose sight of Me. If you revisit a painful memory, remember that I brought it forth so you can forgive, heal, and release it in order to grow and make room for the plans I have for you. Trusting the path that I have placed you on will increase your Faith and give you the Courage to continue on your journey.

I want you to come from Love because it is then that your willing heart opens up to the plans I have for you. I'll meet you right where you're at, always ready to hold your hands and give you the Courage to continue along your Path with ease and grace. The Path will be well-lit as I guide your footsteps to where I want you to be. My unconditional Love will give you the Peace and the Courage you need for the journey. I have overcome the world, you must live in it. My Word is tried and true so stay focused on My face and My promises. Trust in Me as I Trust in You to keep your graceful pace on your scenic and well-lit path that lies ahead.

☦

"Thy word is a lamp unto my feet, and a light unto my path."
Psalms 119:105

"Preserve me, O God: for in thee do I put my trust. Thou wilt shew me the path of life: in thy presence is fullness of joy; at thy right hand there are pleasures for evermore."
Psalms 16:1 & 11

KEEP YOUR EYES ON JESUS

Your Faith will keep you moving forward. Never Give Up because Jesus never does on you. He will meet you right where you are at without any judgments. His unconditional Love and Forgiveness will encompass your heart and mind giving you a Peace that is unmatched. The Lord will Bless you and keep you in His safe and Loving arms if you put Him first. Praise His Holy name and Trust that He will put you right where you need to be. It may not be where you envisioned it, or when you had planned on it, but His Plans and His Timing cannot be questioned. Thy will be done in earth as it is in heaven.

Keep your eyes on Jesus no matter what is going on around you. Do not be moved by your circumstances. God wants you to Trust Him more than ever in the eye of the storm! He is Your Guide and He will light the way and lead the way. As you press in, you press on! Your storms are the time to lean on Him, listen to Him, and build your Trust in Him. Your circumstances can cause you to lose your focus on Him, which is merely a tactic used by the enemy to try and keep you out of Peace and His plans for you. God wants to guide you, Bless you, and carry you through your storms. God's plans are to light your path, lead the way, and give you the Peace, Strength, and clarity to persevere.

God has His Hand in all of it. Pray and cry out to Him, for He is The Comforter, The Healer, and The Provider of all your needs by His riches in glory. Nothing is impossible for God and all things can be overcome. You know the outcome, You are Redeemed and Victorious through Christ Jesus! Continue to put Him first, Trust His plans, and keep your eyes on Him!

✝

"I know thy works; behold, I have set before thee an open door, and no man can shut it: for thou hast a little strength, and hast kept my word, and hast not denied my name."

Revelations 3:8

"And Jesus answering saith unto them, Have faith in God. For verily I say unto you, That whosoever shall say unto this mountain, Be thou removed, and be thou cast into the sea; and shall not doubt in his heart, but shall believe that those things which he saith shall come to pass; he shall have whatsoever he saith. Therefore I say unto you, What things soever ye desire when ye pray, believe that ye receive them, and ye shall have them."

Matthew 11:22-24

I LIFT YOU UP MY CHILD

I lift you up My Child, out of the muck and mire and the depths of what you think is a heart filled with joy, but instead filled with pain and rejection from a past well known. I lift you up My Child, from a place of grief and silent suffering to a place of Joy and encouragement. I lift you up to a place of comfort from a healed heart that is mended when you embrace and receive the unconditional Love I have for you!

I lift you up My Child on this day, to Heal, Let Go, Receive, Give, Love, and feel the place of Peace in your heart that I am mending. Do not be afraid of what is to come. You are an Overcomer! Trust in Me and walk into the divine place I have prepared for you because it is what your soul needs to heal. Walk with ease and grace and share your Joy from your mended heart. You are safe with Me now and forevermore. Be an example of what true Love is and share the Truth of My Son Jesus Christ who lives and reigns with you forever and ever.

Spread your Love from your healed heart. Spread My Light, My Word, and bring Peace to those who need it most. Sharing your journey with Me can encourage others to do the same. Your Courage to reach out and take my hand was meant for you to build your Trust in Me. You are Chosen and You are Worthy! I lift you up My Child for I will never leave you or forsake you.

✝

"I WAITED patiently for the Lord; and He inclined unto me, and heard my cry. He brought me up also out of an horrible pit, out of the miry clay, and set my foot upon a rock, and established my goings. And He hath put a new song in my mouth, even praise unto our God: many shall see it, and fear, and shall trust in the Lord."

Psalms 40:1-3

"Jesus saith unto him, I am the way, the truth, and the life: no man cometh unto the father, but by me."

John 14:6

RISE UP AND RENEW

R ise up out of the wilderness and wickedness and renew the spirit of your mind. That old man, old anger, and old ways of dealing with your life must change. The world system does not serve you anymore. Open up your willing heart to your Heavenly Father and let Him light the way for you. Yield, be still, and let His voice be all that you hear to guide you. His Words will give you Hope and your Faith will give you the Courage to explore what He has on the horizon. Keep your eyes and mind on Jesus and let Him lead the way.

How you see yourself is completely different than how He sees you. God looks on the heart. Your images of treachery and circumstances tend to overshadow your thoughts and vision, keeping you stagnant both emotionally and physically. It is the continuous ploy of the enemy to keep you distracted, over-whelmed, and feeling stuck. The conscious effort to change your mindset and your prayers can become exhausting. When your battles seem endless and your results unchanged, renew your prayers and remember that your prayers do not come back void. The Lord is always listening and He is always with you! He will guide you and give you the Courage to rise up and take another step forward even when you think you can't. Leaning on Him will renew your Strength and keep you going in His Divine direction.

Your Love for Him will renew your Hope and bring you Peace. His unconditional Love for you will give you the stability you need to rise up and walk with Jesus. Be Grateful, for on this day your Lord and Savior will continue to light the way, renew your spirit, and fill you with His everlasting Love and Peace. He will show you a new way to learn by coming from Love and Gratitude. He will renew your life if you allow Him in and are willing to let Him raise you up.

✝

"Arise, shine; for thy light is come, and the glory of the Lord is risen upon thee."

Isaiah 60:1

"For by grace are ye saved through faith; and not that of yourselves: it is the gift of God: Not of works, lest any man should boast. For we are His workmanship, created in Christ Jesus unto good works, which God hath before ordained that we should walk in them."

Ephesians 2:8 & 9

PATIENCE

Being patient requires you to sit still in a place of Peace and there you'll find God always in the center of it. When you are waiting on Him and listening with a willing heart and mind, your timelines and to-do lists must be put aside. Do not prolong the painful process of getting the same results by an unchanged heart and your own agenda. Your patience is required to allow His plans and His timing to place you on the right path to His Divine destination.

How will you learn patience and Faith when you get every-thing immediately? Let go of trying to get what you want, when you want it. A true test of Faith is to wait on the Lord and not lose Hope, even when your prayers feel as though they're going unanswered. While you are patiently praying, you can also learn so many lessons about the importance of what you are asking for. Suddenly your priorities and impatience can turn into a Faith building moment that gives you clarity and wisdom. "Watch and learn" can be part of your Faith building process. A simple observation and repenting can bring you to a place of humility, allowing your pride to vanish and your eyes to be opened. When your path seems to lead to a place that you didn't plan for, Trust that there is something for you to see and be ready to learn. The Lord will orchestrate everything and He will teach you to Trust in His Divine timing. It is in your waiting and wanting that you learn what His plans are for you. As the road becomes more treacherous or seems like it has come to a dead end, God will reward your patience and provide a Blessing to give you the perseverance to carry on. Being an example of Hope may bring a crowd of contenders who have their doubts, but your Obedience and Faith in Him will be recognized, encouraging those who need it most. His promises and rewards can restore Hope in a dying world. Surge forward discerning who is leading you and the light you are sharing on your path to righteousness. Your trail of unforgettable endurance and Faith may inspire and Bless others along their pathway too.

Your patience will always be tested but your Faith will continue to surface when you yield and let His Divine timing be your guide. The Lord has ordered your footsteps and created a scenic path for you to walk on. He will light the way and give you the stamina to endure while providing all of your needs by His riches in Glory. Your patience will Strengthen your Faith when you Trust in Him and pray without ceasing through any storm. Be Grateful for His Guidance, unconditional Love, Divine Delays, and all you have seen and learned along your path. Blessings come to those who Believe, Trust, and patiently wait on The Lord!

✝

"Behold, we count them happy which endure. Ye have heard of the patience of Job, and have seen the end of the Lord; that the Lord is very pitiful, and of tender mercy."
James 5:11

"But they that wait upon the Lord shall renew their strength; they shall mount up with wings as eagles; they shall run, and not be weary; and they shall walk, and not faint."
Isaiah 40:31

OBEDIENCE

Obedience requires your Patience, Perseverance, and Faith. When you decide to listen to the Lord and surrender to His plans for you, Strength and clarity will be your reward. He will give you the Courage to continue if you Trust in Him and His lead. There is a learning curve in the life we choose and your daily choices require you to listen to Him. When you hear Him and step out in Faith, your flesh will try and fight back and retreat to old ways and habits. A way to deny your flesh is not listening to the lies that once fed your soul. A soul that is driven by the wrong spirit will never have peace.

The battle begins in the mind. The lies from the enemy can entrap you to keep you hostage in that familiar place where you get distracted and lose Hope; a ploy so you lose sight of where God wants you to be. Don't allow it to be an excuse to be disobedient. Stay focused on The Lord without backsliding into a lifestyle that once seemed so comfortable. The enemy always tries to entice you and lure you back in with temptations and your familiar dark detours that are around every corner. Take down your flesh by taking over your mind, a task that takes complete Obedience and a conscious effort throughout your day. Your words speak the abundance of your heart and are a test of your Faith. Speak life over everything because the tongue is a little member, and boasts great things.

Fasting, praying, and asking the Lord for more of Him and less of you, will reap great rewards for your Obedience. When you visit old places, you don't have to revert back to old thoughts and old ways. Break those chains of bondage and allow God in so He can heal you!

Obedience requires you to be still and patient even when you want to run down your own path. Sometimes you may be running away from His Blessings and the desires of your heart. Stand in Faith and overcome your fear of what you think you will lose or may have to let go of. When you are listening to Him, Trust that He will reward you for your perseverance and Obedience. Never give up or lose Hope. Your patience allows you to be humbled, learn valuable lessons, and truly appreciate His timing and His Blessings even more. What you learn in the waiting and the wanting also increases your Faith.

Seek Him first and allow Him to place you where He wants you to be. Listen, choose to be Obedient, and have Faith that the footsteps He has ordered for you are filled with Abundant Blessings. Don't look back on where you traveled from instead look forward knowing He is guiding you in His Divine direction. Keep your eyes on Him, listen to His voice, and Trust that God always rewards Obedience.

"But whoso keepeth His word, in Him verily is the love of the God perfected: hereby know we that we are in Him."
1 John 2:5

"Behold, happy is the man whom God correcteth: therefore despise not the chastening of the Almighty: For He maketh sore, and bindeth up: He woundeth, and His hands make whole."

Job 5:17 & 18

LET GOD LEAD

In order to be led you must be willing to surrender and give everything to God. Your thoughts, your timelines, your plans, and your ways don't allow Him to lead you. Let go and leave your distracted and worried mind behind. He will meet you right where you're at. Be ready to receive His hand in Trust and allow Him to lead you to where He has prepared for you. The Peaceful path that lies ahead doesn't take a controlling thought to make its way forward. Trust in His timing and allow Him to lead the way. He knows the way because He paved the way and it is perfectly timed and mapped out for your success. Keep your eyes on Him and not on what lies ahead with anticipation and anxiousness. If fear arises in you, know that it is not Him but the enemy who wants to distract you so you miss the Blessings in disguise.

Your circumstances are mere distractions and if you don't surrender and allow God to guide you they will overwhelm you. Lean on Him and follow Him on every mountain that you must climb. His timing is part of the lesson in your Faith that must be learned before another step is taken. He'll give you the Courage and Strength to overcome any obstacle so you can reach the mountain tops. Give all the Glory to God upon arrival and His Blessings will continue to flow and lead you to where He wants you to be.

There will be doors that will open and some that will shut. Trust that He is closing the doors and removing the people that need to be removed. This is all a part of your journey to build your Trust in Him and guide you to the Blessings He has in store for you. Surrendering to Him is not giving in or giving up but Trusting that He's leading you along your well-lit path.

Washing with the water of the Word will help keep your focus on Him, and your thoughts on His Truth and His Promises. Your willing heart will be able to receive His unconditional Love that will keep you in Peace and yielding to His voice. Get Rest, Rejuvenate, and Rejoice in knowing that His Hand is upon you, pushing you to the peaks, carrying you through the valleys, and leading you to the doors that He may open or close. When you finally let go of the reigns and surrender it all to Him, then you can take His hand and He will lead you to your Divine Destiny.

"For we walk by Faith, not by sight..."
$\qquad$ *2 Corinthians 5:7*

"The steps of a good man are ordered by the Lord: and He delighteth in his way."
$\qquad$ *Psalm 37:23*

DIVINE DELAY

A Divine Delay is all part of God's Plan. Surrender and allow His timing and His plans to override yours. He sees your willing heart and knows when the time is right to proceed or receive a Blessing. When your plans don't go your way, listen to His voice and Trust Him without wavering in your Faith. Yield, pray, and get out of the way so you're able to see how God has orchestrated His Divine plans for you.

Relinquish what you think is yours to control. Letting go of a thought, the process, and the timing of your plans can be very difficult. Once you can surrender everything to Him, that is when your journey of Faith begins. When you finally Trust in His timing, you can take comfort in knowing that He has it all in His Hands. A delay is not denial! A delay is God working on your behalf as He puts everything into Divine order. This is your time to be still as your patience and Faith in Him are being tested. As you lean on Him and Trust what He is doing, your Faith is building. How you've envisioned it always seems to be different than how and when He presents it. A Divine Delay is the opportunity for your Faith to override any doubts or fears. Surrendering allows you to receive His Divine timeline and His Blessings.

Throughout the many trials you will face and tears that you'll shed, your willing heart must always Trust in His timing. Your test of patience can seem never ending but continue to Pray without ceasing and stand strong on His Word and His Promises. Speak life as you wait in joyful Hope for what the Lord is doing. Trust that He will break any strongholds if that's what is needed. He will shut a door, or remove a person that tries to block your Blessings and is merely a distraction. While you don't know what He is doing or what lies ahead, there is no better way to build your Faith then by letting go and giving it all to God. Trust in all of His Divine Delays and His Divine plans along your well-lit path. Continue to keep your eyes on Him and stay in a place of Peace regardless of your circumstances. Trust that His Divine Timing is perfect in all things.

"And He said unto them, It is not for you to know the times or the seasons, which the Father hath put in His own power."

Acts 1:7

"And let us not be weary in well doing: for in due season we shall reap, if we faint not."

Galations 6:9

A WALK OF FAITH

A Walk of Faith may not feel like a walk at all but more like a treacherous climb up the face of a steep mountain. Once your feet think they've hit some solid ground, the walk continues and is filled with various circumstances and scenery. This walk may either distract you or allow you to continue to focus on The Lord. There is also barren ground that one day will bring you the fruits of your labor. Green patches can be seen where seeds have been planted with a word spoken in season.

Be alert to the roadblocks that lie ahead and Trust that you can overcome them with your Godly wisdom. Your discernment was acquired as you climbed the mountains and crossed through the empty fields. In your moments when life seems to stand still, God will give you the Strength to move forward and Walk in Faith if you let Him. Through the vastness and pain, continue to stay in His Word allowing Him to plant scriptures in your heart and Peace to cling to. His unconditional Love and mercy are what you need to Thank Him for; not just when you reach the mountain tops or when look at your green pastures, but also when the ground was barren and your trials seemed never ending.

Walking in Faith is no easy walk and takes unexplainable perseverance and Courage to continue down your path to what lies ahead. It takes Courage not to get discouraged. Pour your Faith into Him and rely on His promises and His light to guide your next steps. There are no limits to your prayers, God can do the impossible! If you are Obedient and rely on Him, He will never cease to amaze you and will continue to guide your footsteps of Faith.

Be ready to receive the Holy Spirit and allow it to work through you. You will then move at His Peaceful pace with ease and grace. A Walk of Faith is led by the Holy Spirit who safely embraces your heart and hands leading you to His Holy place of Peace. Your perseverance will encourage others as they come to know The Lord remembering the Strength He gave you. Their eyes will be opened up to a world that He wants them to see. Walking in Faith and sharing your joy through all of your storms can bring Hope for the many souls that need to be Saved. The onlookers may be stumbling on their walk and wavering in their Faith but your graceful pace will shine forth and inspire those who cross your path. Observing your footsteps that are filled with Love and Hope may be just what they need to see to keep moving forward in Faith. Your journey with Jesus may not always be easy but the smallest amount of Faith won't be over-looked or measured. Never underestimate the power of God's will in your life. As He takes your hand to gracefully guide you, grip it tight and walk in Faith knowing that He is always with you and will light the way.

"*Now faith is the substance of things hoped for, the evidence of things not seen.*"

Hebrews 11:1

"And Jesus said unto them, Because of your unbelief: for verily I say unto you, If ye have faith as a grain of mustard seed, ye shall say unto this mountain, Remove hence to yonder place; and it shall remove; and nothing shall be impossible unto you."

Matthew 17:20

HOPE

Hope in the Lord is all we have when we are facing the impossible. Never lose Hope during any kind of storm! If you feel like you can't take another step, He will give you the Courage to move forward and take your hand to guide you, or carry you the rest of the way. His unending Love for you is the Strength you need to persevere, even when you think you can't. Your Hope in Him gives you Strength by relying on His Word and His promises to grow and prosper.

Have Hope in knowing that as you stand on your unstable ground, God's roots have you firmly planted in His garden of goodness. There are times when your life may feel like a vine blowing in the wind that's desperately trying to grow in the earth's vastness of a desolate field. When your vine is reaching out to grasp what seems like thin air, it is then that your test of Faith begins. Never lose Hope and Trust that God's hands will stretch forth to take hold of yours. His gentleness and rich soil are always ready to take a seed and spring forth life. A mustard seed grows into a plant that doesn't seem to match its starting point. God knows the end result and His plans for you, therefore your Hope must not waver in any storm. Although it may be treacherous at times, you must always Trust in the Lord and keep your eyes on Him. God's soil is rich and filled with His Words of Wisdom, Hope, and His promises. Keep your Faith firmly planted in God's garden when you are weary and hope-less, the soil is filled with His plans and His promises. Your roots will start to grow when your Trust in Him abounds in your heart.

As you get out of His way, He sheds the light you need to see to make your way forward. God's Love and Strength that has car-ried you through your storms and given you Hope may be the example a troubled one yearns to see. There are people around every corner who need a ray of Hope, a Word in season, or a Blessing from above. You may be their only example of Hope in guiding them to Him. Your storm may be similar to theirs and knowing that you persevered without giving up Hope can be their stepping stone of Faith. God may have put you through your storms to give you the compassion to help someone else through theirs. Be careful not to discourage but to encourage those in need, for their path may have only led to dead ends until now. Never miss an opportunity to share the Love He has shared with you. Being a beacon of light for someone during their storm takes a moment if your heart is pure and willing to give a word in season.

Be mindful of who has planted your seed, enriched your soil, and guided you through the many storms in your life. Thank the Lord for giving you Hope and enriching your soil to grow with Strength, Courage, and Compassion. His unconditional Love is a gift that can always be opened whenever your heart needs Hope to continue along your journey. He paid the price for you when He died on the cross, and then miraculously rose from the dead. Have Hope and remember the ultimate sacrifice your Lord and Savior Jesus Christ made. Always Believe that you are Worthy to receive His Blessings and that your Hope in Him is everything you will ever need to continue through your storms!

*"Now the God of hope fill you with all joy and peace in
believing that ye may abound in hope, through the power
of the Holy Ghost."*

Roman 15:13

*"Be of good courage, and He shall strengthen your heart,
all ye that hope in the Lord."*

Psalm 31:24

TRUST

Trusting God when your circumstances are chaotic is truly one of the hardest parts in your Walk of Faith. It's easy to get distracted and lose sight of God. Where He wants you, may not match where you envisioned you wanted to be. The enemy comes in and dims the light on your path and keeps the lies coming in. You can become comfortable being stuck in an old mindset and ways that never get you anywhere. You may find comfort in the deception that you are not worthy to move forward and have what you deserve. Some days those lies are all that you seem to hear. Be still, let go, and listen for The Lord's voice. The ability to take a moment to pray and hear Him will be worth it. Surrender and Trust that He is trying to show you that His plans and His Timing are more Blessed than your timelines.

What are you hanging on to? Purge out the old for there is nothing but a split second when all will be left behind. Trust the path He has put you on and stop maneuvering and manipulating to get where you want. Trying to control your destination is the first thing you need to let go of. How are you Trusting Him if you are doing all of the navigating? He met you right where you were at, Trust that He will place you right where you are supposed to be. If you are a new creature in Christ, the ungodly and unsightly will not be fulfilling to your spirit anymore. Trust the journey realizing that He knows what is best and He wants to Bless You! He will deliver His promises and answer your prayers but you must Trust in His Timing.

He will get your attention and bring you to your knees if He has to. Your trials and tribulations are your opportunity to lean on Him and build your Faith. Believe that He will make a way where there is no way. He will raise you up out of any storm, if you let Him. He is listening to your prayers, are you hearing Him answer? He will wait for you to open up your willing heart and eyes to His purpose for you. He will show you He is with you when you finally yield and push your thoughts and ways aside. It is up to you to decide to make time for Him, listen for His voice, be Obedient, and pray without ceasing. It is up to you to Trust His plans and that He will move you through your day at a graceful pace. He will show you which door to walk through and which door to shut. He has ordered your footsteps and the promises of a life filled with unimaginable Love and abundant Blessings.

While your path also includes many trials and fiery storms, they are your true tests of perseverance and Faith. Trust Him enough to give it all to Him! Don't try to get ahead of Him and the plans He has for You, Trust that He will deliver in His Perfect Timing. Any Divine Delays are His Way of getting everything into Divine order. You can't get discouraged if the path changes direction. The Lord has His Way of guiding you to where He wants you to be. Trust the direction you're going and what He wants you to see and learn along the way. He is with you through all of it, providing the Strength and Courage to endure. The closer you are getting to a Blessing, the harder the enemy tries to distract you and destroy your Hopes and dreams. Never Give Up! Keep moving forward conquering your fears and any doubts. Open up your willing heart and mind to embrace the Love He has for you and the Faith He has in you. You must do the same for Him! Keep your eyes fixed on Him and move forward with anticipation of more Love, mercy, grace, forgiveness, and guidance.

Always be Grateful and accept where He places you on your path. There is always something to learn on your journey with Jesus. Trust in His Timing, His Will, and The Way He has prepared for you. Listen and Believe that He will guide your footsteps in His Divine Direction with ease and grace. Your vulnerable moments of walking in Faith will become your Victorious moments when you Trust in Him!

"Trust in the Lord with all thine heart; and lean not unto thine own understanding. In all thy ways acknowledge Him, and He shall direct thy paths."

Proverbs 3:5 & 6

"Every word of God is pure: He is a shield unto them that put their trust in Him."

Proverbs 30:5

FAITH BRINGS HOPE

F inding Peace is having Faith in Me. I am the one you can depend on to set you free from the distractions and temptations of this world. My efforts for you to feel my unconditional Love in your time of need can get pushed aside because of your sinful nature that finds pleasure in a world that feeds your soul. The Holy Spirit, when aligned with the Truth, will not be fed in this world anymore. My Love, My Light, and My Word will fill your Spirit to a Peaceful place of serenity. While your trials may seem never ending, you can always rely on Me and My Word to give you the Strength that you need for the journey.

Let your focus be on your Faith in Me for it is the way to everlasting Peace. Be still and always know that My Strength and your Faith will sustain you. Your Faith can be measured by how you handle your circumstances. Your Hope must not waver and you cannot be moved. Allow My unconditional Love and My Promises to encompass your heart and your mind. Hope in Me will sustain you and My Word will give you Peace. The Blessings I have in store for you will be revealed as you continue to walk by Faith and not by sight.

Spreading my light that is abounding inside of you can be seen by others with a curious eye. Saying it is "Jesus" can bring Joy, for my Son is everyone's ray of Hope during a dark time. Be

My hands of Hope to the one who is reaching for Me. Sharing a Word in season may only take a moment but it will continue to resonate in their heart much longer. It can come back to remembrance when their prayers seem to be going unanswered. Be a beacon of light to gently guide them to Me, the place of unconditional Love and comfort that their soul longs for. As you try to encourage others, the focus off yourself sheds a new light on your needs and their importance. Be a Blessing to others and speak life over everything. Being of service and ministering to others is an important part of Strengthening your Faith on your journey. Your test of perseverance will bring Hope to those who stand on My Word and Believe in Me.

"And ye shall know the truth, and the truth shall make you free."

John 8:32

"So shall my word be that goeth forth out of my mouth: it shall not return unto me void, but it shall accomplish that which I please, and it shall prosper in the thing whereto I sent it."

Isaiah 55:11

THE ENEMY

Y ou must put on your armor every single day! The enemy is roaming around like a lion trying any tactic, preying on your weaknesses, and will use anything he can to cause division, confusion, worry, doubt, depression, anxiety, unworthiness, fear, anger, temptation, and the list goes on. The enemy is a liar! You must stand strong in your Faith and not be overtaken by his wickedness. The battle begins in the mind. Your thoughts must not wander down that dark hallway into the abyss of the enemy's lies, negativity, and fear. Living a life of temptation and sin will lead you into the darkness. The Lord is a lamp unto your feet. He will light the way and give you the Strength, Hope, and Courage to resist the snares of the enemy and fight the good fight of Faith.

You are going to come up against darkness, trials, and people that are not in line with God's Word. You need to be aware of who it is that tries to overtake your thoughts, your words, and your actions; for it is then that you must proclaim Jesus Christ is your Lord and Savior and speak out against any form of the enemy. He can use people to try and cause division, distractions, confusion, and fear. Once you are in fear, you can be easily overtaken and controlled. You must be aware of his plans to blindside you at any moment because he comes to kill, steal, and destroy. Keep your eyes on The Lord for He will never leave you or forsake you. His Word is the armor that you need to win the battle and overtake the fear, the lies, and the chaos. The enemy doesn't sleep so you must continually put him behind you and under your feet! Speak out against him whenever you are under attack. Tell him to back off and let him know that you aren't listening to his lies!

The days of running yourself into the ground to the point of exhaustion must come to an end. Fatigue is an opportunity for the enemy to try and overtake you, recognizing that your fight may not be as strong. Get rest and Stand Strong on God's Word and Promises. Take care of your vessel for you house the Holy Spirit inside of you. Let the scriptures settle into your mind and walk in God's Grace recognizing that your armor needs to be worn at all times.

Remember that you don't wrestle against flesh and blood, but against powers and principalities. Your discernment is needed at all times because the enemy is constantly trying to steal your Peace. What voice you listen to is a choice. Staying in Peace is a choice. Learning to stand on God's Word is also a choice. Choose wisely because a wavering soul is the enemy's playground.

Unyielding in your Faith and Trusting in God's Word will help you to persevere through your trials without giving in to temptations. Don't allow distractions and your circumstances to cause you to lose focus and take a detour into darkness. Stand firm and keep your eyes on The Lord. Always remember that He is still on The Throne and that You Are Victorious through Christ Jesus! Period.

☦

"For God hath not given us a spirit of fear; but of power, and of love, and of a sound mind."
2 Timothy 1:7

45

"Put on the whole armor of God, that ye may be able to stand against the wiles of the devil. For we wrestle not against flesh and blood, but against principalities, against powers, against the rulers of the darkness of this world, against spiritual wickedness in high places."

Ephesians 6:11 & 12

"For God is not the author of confusion, but of peace, as in all churches of the saints."

1 Corinthians 14:33

NOW IS THE TIME

N ow is the time when temptation will be overtaken by your determination to stay on track and not be swayed. You have to walk away from whatever the enemy tries to lure you in with. The intrigue and the lies that "it's ok" will not fly anymore. The time is now to step-up to the plate and swing away at all of the deception, distractions, and arrows that are thrown your way. Now is the time when consequences will be taken to heart and the impact of your prior mishaps and decisions will be learned from; any sooner, and the lesson would have no worth, no impact, and regarded resentfully.

True forgiveness is forgiving yourself and knowing that God has forgiven you. Reflecting on a decision made on impulse and loathing in self-condemnation and unworthiness is exactly where the enemy wants you to remain. He wreaks havoc and will keep you in emotional bondage as long as he can. Standing on God's Word and the wisdom that He has taught you will give you the steadfastness to turn a cheek to anything that is not of Him. Stand strong in your Faith and know that your Obedience is an ongoing test on your path.

The time is now to put on the armor of God knowing that He will work on your behalf. God will give you the Strength to deflect the arrows, distractions, and the lies to help you discern what is not of Him. He will guide you along your well-lit path if you get out of the way and let Him lead.

The time is now to fight the good fight of Faith, walk away from temptations, and pray without ceasing! Your redemption time is a result of your Faithfulness and Obedience. Know that now is the time that He will reward you openly and those who diligently seek Him first.

☩

"We love Him, because He first loved us."

1 John 4:19

"What time I am afraid, I will trust in thee. In God I will praise His word, in God I have put my Trust: I will not fear what flesh can do unto me."

Psalms 56:3 & 4

MY WAYS

My Ways aren't meant for you to understand but your time to surrender to Me. Your ways and actions are not to be reactions or resistance, but Trusting that I have ordered your footsteps to a Divine destination. Your new pace will awaken you to find that it is filled with ease and grace. A driving spirit will deplete you and your ability to focus on Me. When you listen and yield to Me, My Word will come forth and be the answer that you need.

Humble yourself and let My Presence be felt in your moments of discontent. The drive to do all that needs to be done will take a different turn now, for in My timing, needs are met and timelines are gone. My Ways are not always what you imagine but if keep your focus on Me, I will help you accomplish the task at hand.

Your ways can paint a picture that may not be easy to look at. Let your canvas be filled with the abundant Blessings to come that only I will provide. There are times when My Ways may not be understood. That day in Calvary when my Son was crucified and all seemed too excruciatingly painful and hopeless to endure, My Way to everlasting life was My answer.

Questioning how things are unfolding shows your lack of Trust in Me. Your Faith building times are when you are leaning on Me and Trusting that My Ways are the only way. My plans are to guide you, protect you, and Bless you. Your plans can be to yield, listen, and have Hope that I have it all in hand. I have chosen foolish things to confound the wise. Trust My Ways and know that My Will shall be done in earth as it is in heaven. Have Faith in Me knowing that I will always be with you and that My Ways are what is best for you.

"For My thoughts are not your thoughts, neither are your ways My ways, saith the Lord. For as the heavens are higher than the earth, so are My ways higher than your ways, and my thoughts than your thoughts."

Isaiah 55:8 & 9

"But the wisdom that is from above is first pure, then peaceable, gentle, and easy to be intreated, full of mercy and good fruits, without partiality, and without hypocrisy. And the fruit of righteousness is sown in peace of them that make peace."

James 3:17 & 18

FAITH

Faith building begins when your plans end and you are able to surrender everything to your Heavenly Father. Faith is a never ending test of your patience and perseverance. Your fiery trials will help you to build your Faith and relationship with Him. You must have Faith in Him at all times. His Love never fails and your Faith and Love for Him should not waver in your storms. You can't ask why, for in the asking He knows that you don't Trust in Him. Surrendering everything to Him shows that you are His to work on, and work with. He needs your willing heart to remain Faithful to His plans for you.

Trust Him to guide you to His place of Peace which requires you to open your willing heart to His Ways. You can't look at your circumstances because in the natural world they may seem dire. Your Faith will bring you Peace if you can keep a steadfast gaze on Him. When your Faith wavers you must remember that He is with you, even when it seems He is silent and your prayers are going unanswered. Have Faith and know that He will never leave you or forsake you. Continue to pray during the storms that you face. If you don't see a change, adjust your prayers and ask God to search your heart to remove any anger, resentment, and lack of patience or forgiveness. Your heart cannot house any bitterness because it can block your Blessings. Let go of a past that doesn't serve you but only blurs your vision of Jesus and hardens your heart.

Trust in His Will and His Timing and remain in a place of Gratitude knowing that any opportunity to lean on Him is a Blessing. There are Blessings even in the trials, so move forward in Faith knowing that whatever lies ahead on your path is what He wants for you. Your fears have to be overcome by Your Faith!

Faith is not being able to see where He is taking you. Trust that the Lord has His hand upon you, guiding you and leading the way. Faith is the confidence in knowing that what God has in store for you is what is best for you. Have patience and Faith in His Divine order, Trust His Perfect Plan, and His Perfect Timing. His Love never fails and your Faith shouldn't either. Let your storms be nothing but a passing cloud that lifted to give you the clarity you needed and to leave an indelible mark of Courage that increases your Faith. You must allow your Faith in Him to get stronger even through the trials. No matter what you are facing, God is bigger than all of it! There's not a storm He can't see you through, or mountain too high to climb. He will carry you if you get weary and provide the Strength to endure what you think you can't. Ask and you shall receive remembering that He is the Miracle Worker. Have Faith in knowing that you can overcome anything because nothing is impossible for God!

"Rejoice evermore. Pray without ceasing. In every thing give thanks: for this is the will of God in Christ Jesus concerning you."

1 Thessalonians 5:16-18

"I am crucified with Christ: nevertheless I live: yet not I, but Christ liveth in me: and the life which I now live in the flesh I live by the Faith of the Son of God, who loved me, and gave himself for me."

Galatians 2:20

A FORGIVING HEART

A forgiving heart is a healing heart. Forgive, let go, and move forward in Love. My unconditional Love for you will shine through if your unforgiveness can be part of your past. Lack of forgiveness can lead to bitterness and resentment and in order to heal, it cannot occupy any space in your heart or mind. Letting go of the pain can make room in your heart to fill the voids with My Love and Forgiveness. Leave it all behind to allow your willing heart to be repaired. Old thoughts and old ways are part of a past that needs to be reconciled and released. Forgiving yourself is also part of the healing process. Don't allow the enemy to hold your heart hostage. Yesterday is over but if you're looking back on your plow you'll miss the Blessings I have in store for you. Be ready for a new beginning that is free of burdens and the emotional baggage that can block My Blessings for you.

Look forward on your path with Hope and resilience while keeping your focus on Me. Look ahead with a willing heart that yearns for My unconditional Love and My Word that will give you Strength and Courage. I will pour My Joy and Peace into your empty heart that needs to be healed and know the Truth. Fear not, for I am by your side to help you overcome the peace stealers. My Words are always with you, unlike a weapon that can be stripped and leave you feeling helpless. A swordsman in battle relies on his precise training, but once stripped of his sword his training is of no use. Your study of My Word will never leave you, nor will I. I will be with you until we meet again in eternity, flying high above the worries of the world that can try to overtake you. My Mercy is given and you are Forgiven. Feel the weights being lifted off of your heart as you Forgive those who have deceived you. Be at Peace my child, for it is there that your pure and forgiving heart will shine forth and encourage others to seek the Truth of My Word and My unconditional Love.

"Every way of a man is right in his own eyes; but the Lord pondereth the hearts."

Proverbs 18:15

"After this manner therefore pray ye: Our Father which art in heaven, Hallowed be thy name. Thy kingdom come. Thy will be done in earth, as it is in heaven. Give us this day our daily bread. And forgive us our debts, as we forgive our debtors. And lead us not into temptation, but deliver us from evil: For thine is the kingdom, and the power, and the glory, for ever, A-men. For if ye forgive men their trespasses, your Heavenly Father will also forgive you. But if ye forgive not men their trespasses, neither will your Father forgive your trespasses."

Matthew 6:9-15

A NEW BOOK

You are so Blessed to have such an Amazing Author and Finisher in your own Book of Life. The pages are filled with memories that will hold true to your heart and keep you wanting to open to the next chapter. Some pages may help you reflect on a part of your path that gave you the Strength and Courage to start a new chapter. There are other pages that are meant to be written, lived, and forgotten. Opening up an old book may resurrect old pain. While some images may be beautiful, the underlying memories of sadness may be the only thing your heart feels and you see. The lesson learned, the knowledge gained, and the Faith to carry on is what should be brought back to remembrance. Not all books need to be read more than once.

The time will come to start a new book and choose a new title. Look forward to the new pages to come. The Lord will be on the Journey with you, guiding you and giving you the Love and Peace your heart needs. It is your choice what will go on those pages and to listen to God and what He has in store for you. His words of Life, words of Hope, and words of Faith are all words to live by. It is up to you to speak His words and speak life over everything. Life and death are in the power of the tongue. The mouth speaks the abundance of the heart and you must know the power of your words! If your prayers seem to be going unanswered and the chapters aren't changing, change your prayers and speak life over what you want. God looks on the heart, be aware of what is stored in it. Forgive, Let Go, and Believe that your pages to come will be a reflection of being a new creature in Christ.

Enjoy your new book with its new pages, new chapters, and the treasured memories they will bring. Have Faith in knowing that the unconditional Love and sacred time with Jesus will be a part of every page.

✝

"But thanks be to God, which giveth us the victory through our Lord Jesus Christ. Therefore, my beloved brethren, be ye steadfast, unmoveable, always abounding in the work of the Lord, forasmuch as ye know that your labour is not in vain in the Lord."
1 Corinthians 15:57 & 58

"Therefore if any man be in Christ, he is a new creature: old things are passed away; behold, all things are become new."
2 Corinthians 5:17

ON YOUR JOURNEY
WITH JESUS

❦

May you dig deep within yourself
to purify your soul.

May the bumps in the road be a time
of building your Faith.

May the roadblocks not be resented,
but a reminder to Trust in His plans for you.

May His Ways be welcomed, knowing that
His Divine Timing is perfect in all things.

Part 2

May your quiet times inspire you to listen, pray, and write whatever The Lord puts on your heart.

Pray

Rest

Ask

Yield

Endure

Rejoice

Seek

PRAYERS

You have to get out of your own way to be able to see how
God has orchestrated His Divine Plans for you.

PRAYERS

For it is in our darkest hours that His light shines so bright.

PRAYERS

The time is now to fight the good fight of Faith,
walk away from temptation, and pray without ceasing!

PRAYERS

As you press in, you press on.

PRAYERS

Move forward in Faith and come from a place of Love…
Always.

PRAYERS

Your Faith is yours alone, but you are not alone because He is always with you, never leaving you or forsaking you.

PRAYERS

If you revisit a painful experience, then you must release the
pain in order to grow and make room for a new perspective,
and the plans He has for you.

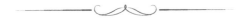

PRAYERS

Trust in Me as I Trust in you.

PRAYERS

God's plans are to Bless you and
carry you through your storms.

PRAYERS

God's Love will endure Forever!

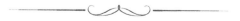

PRAYERS

God always rewards Obedience.

PRAYERS

Your Faith in Him will give you the Strength
you need to rise up, even when you think you can't.

PRAYERS

As hard as it may be to endure, your Gratitude and Trust
in Him will give you the Courage to carry on.

PRAYERS

Your Wisdom and discernment was acquired
when the road seemed so barren and lonely.

PRAYERS

Be aware of who is leading you and the footsteps
you leave on your path to righteousness.

PRAYERS

Humble yourself and let My Presence be
felt in your moments of discontent.

PRAYERS

Hope is knowing that as you stand firmly
on your unstable ground, God's roots have you firmly
planted in His garden of goodness.

PRAYERS

Be careful not to discourage, but to encourage.

PRAYERS

His Mercy is given and You are Forgiven.

PRAYERS

Accept where I have placed you,
for a Grateful heart is a Trusting heart.

PRAYERS

True forgiveness is forgiving yourself
and knowing that God has forgiven you.

PRAYERS

Speak life over everything.

PRAYERS

You know the outcome, You are
Victorious through Christ Jesus!

PRAYERS

God's Love will heal and endure forever!

Gratitude

God looks on the heart.
He wants you to keep your
focus on Him through the
trials, and not on your
circumstances. If you can be
Grateful for the journey
it will bring Peace to your
heart and mind. Gratitude
will bring in Miracles!

I'm GRATEFUL for...

Miracles

I'm GRATEFUL for…

Patience

I'm GRATEFUL for…

Love

I'm GRATEFUL for…

Appreciation

I'm GRATEFUL for…

Laughter

I'm GRATEFUL for...

Joy

I'm GRATEFUL for...

Growth

I'm GRATEFUL for…

Kindness

I'm GRATEFUL for…

Respect

I'm GRATEFUL for…

Mercy

I'm GRATEFUL for…

Forgiveness

I'm GRATEFUL for...

Generosity

I'm GRATEFUL for...

Endurance

I'm GRATEFUL for...

The little things

I'm GRATEFUL for…

Grace

I'm GRATEFUL for…

Hope

I'm GRATEFUL for…

Healing

I'm GRATEFUL for…

Praise

I'm GRATEFUL for...

Courage

I'm GRATEFUL for…

Peace

I'm GRATEFUL for...

Family and Friends

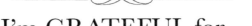

I'm GRATEFUL for…

Victories

I'm GRATEFUL for…

Jesus

Sacred Writings

TAKE TIME
FOR YOURSELF
TO LISTEN AND WRITE
WHAT THE LORD PUTS
ON YOUR HEART.

SACRED WRITINGS

SACRED WRITINGS

SACRED WRITINGS

SACRED WRITINGS

SACRED WRITINGS

SACRED WRITINGS

SACRED WRITINGS

SACRED WRITINGS

SACRED WRITINGS

SACRED WRITINGS

SACRED WRITINGS

SACRED WRITINGS

SACRED WRITINGS

SACRED WRITINGS

SACRED WRITINGS

SACRED WRITINGS

SACRED WRITINGS

SACRED WRITINGS

SACRED WRITINGS

SACRED WRITINGS

SACRED WRITINGS

SACRED WRITINGS

SACRED WRITINGS

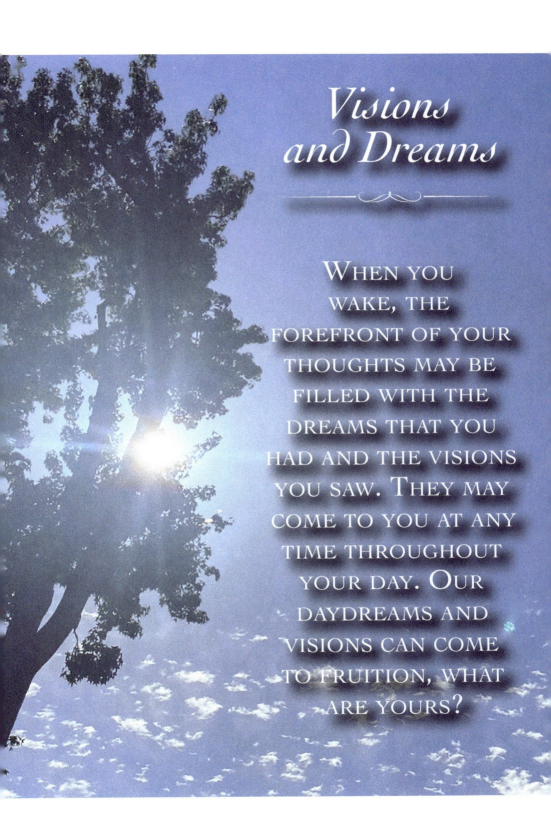

Visions and Dreams

WHEN YOU WAKE, THE FOREFRONT OF YOUR THOUGHTS MAY BE FILLED WITH THE DREAMS THAT YOU HAD AND THE VISIONS YOU SAW. THEY MAY COME TO YOU AT ANY TIME THROUGHOUT YOUR DAY. OUR DAYDREAMS AND VISIONS CAN COME TO FRUITION, WHAT ARE YOURS?

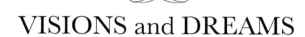

VISIONS and DREAMS

Let Go and Surrender Everything to Him.

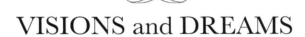

VISIONS and DREAMS

You are Worthy.

VISIONS and DREAMS

You are Blessed and Highly Favored.

VISIONS and DREAMS

You have favor with God and man.

VISIONS and DREAMS

Any opportunity to lean on Him is a Blessing.

VISIONS and DREAMS

God reveals everything in His timing.

VISIONS and DREAMS

Redemption Time

VISIONS and DREAMS

God's Timing is Perfect.

VISIONS and DREAMS

Be Unoffendable

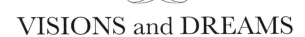

VISIONS and DREAMS

Persevere through the storms.

VISIONS and DREAMS

Let Go and Love

VISIONS and DREAMS

Trust in Him.

VISIONS and DREAMS

Transition Time

VISIONS and DREAMS

Judge Not

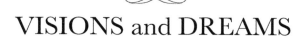

VISIONS and DREAMS

Give and Receive

VISIONS and DREAMS

Forgive others and yourself... Forgiveness is freeing.

VISIONS and DREAMS

Be a Blessing to others.

VISIONS and DREAMS

Pray, Smile and move forward in Faith.

VISIONS and DREAMS

Never Give Up Hope.

VISIONS and DREAMS

Walk with ease and Grace.

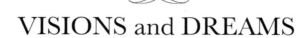

VISIONS and DREAMS

Be Still.

VISIONS and DREAMS

Make a Difference, be the Difference.

VISIONS and DREAMS

You are Victorious through Christ Jesus!

Blessings and Miracles

———⟪⟫———

On your Journey with Jesus there are Blessings and Miracles along your path; reflecting and sharing them with others gives them Hope. Hope is all you need to continue to move forward in Faith. Here's to the many Abundant Blessings and unexplained Miracles that only Jesus can perform.

BLESSINGS and MIRACLES

BLESSINGS and MIRACLES

BLESSINGS and MIRACLES

BLESSINGS and MIRACLES

BLESSINGS and MIRACLES

BLESSINGS and MIRACLES

BLESSINGS and MIRACLES

BLESSINGS and MIRACLES

BLESSINGS and MIRACLES

BLESSINGS and MIRACLES

BLESSINGS and MIRACLES

BLESSINGS and MIRACLES

BLESSINGS and MIRACLES

BLESSINGS and MIRACLES

BLESSINGS and MIRACLES

BLESSINGS and MIRACLES

BLESSINGS and MIRACLES

BLESSINGS and MIRACLES

BLESSINGS and MIRACLES

BLESSINGS and MIRACLES

BLESSINGS and MIRACLES

BLESSINGS and MIRACLES

BLESSINGS and MIRACLES

INTENTIONS

I hope this book has helped you to Be Still, Yield, and Listen to what the Lord puts on your heart. I pray it has lifted your spirit, put you in a place of Gratitude, leads you to Forgive others, including yourself, have Hope, Believe, Appreciate your gifts, and build your Sacred relationship with Him.

If you have any Prayer requests, you can email them to me at: peacenprayers@gmail.com

A portion of the proceeds from this book will go to: NCOSE, a non-profit organization focused on exposing and ending all forms of sexual abuse and exploitation, The Lighthouse - A Place of Refuge, a non-profit organization helping home-less youths and Veterans, Food Pantry's, Clothing and School Supply drives, Animal Rescues, and whatever else God puts on my heart. Giving is Living.

"Let brotherly love continue. Be not forgetful to entertain strangers: for thereby some have entertained angels unawares."

Hebrews 13:1 & 2

"And when he had called the people unto Him with His disciples also, He said unto them, Whosoever will come after me, let him deny himself, and take up his cross, and follow Me. For whosoever will save his life shall lose it; but whosoever shall lose his life for My sake and the gospel's, the same shall save it."

Mark 8:34 & 35

MY JOURNEY

I am the youngest of 6 children and was always floundering in school because it was very difficult for me. I had a hard time focusing and an even harder time comprehending what I read. I preferred to daydream and draw, and play outside at recess. I was always trying my best to avoid making eye contact with the teacher so I wouldn't be called upon. I enjoyed sports, riding bikes, hide-and-seek, and TV tag or freeze tag, and playing only until the street lights came on. I was also very content playing in my playhouse that my Dad and Grandfather built. I would use my imagination playing by myself or alongside a friend. We would spend hours making mud pies and salads out of all the different leaves we would gather. I loved to climb up our lemon tree and find a spot on top of the cinder block wall to gaze over at the neighbor's pool always picturing myself in it. My childhood was spent going to church on Sundays and celebrating Holidays and Birthdays with my large extended family and friends. Unfortunately, I didn't always make the kindest choices in school, possibly out of frustration and getting teased constantly. I was a kid trying to navigate my way through life trying to figure out who I was, without being compared to my studious siblings. For the most part, my life was good but that all ended in the eighth grade, at the age of 13. It was Friday, November 3, 1978 at around 3:15 in the afternoon. I was walking home from school and my Aunt, Uncle, and my oldest Sister parked along the street and they were there to pick me up. I thought it was odd but in my excitement I hopped in the back seat of the car and asked if they were taking me to my doctor appointment. My Sister grabbed me and held me tight as my Aunt turned to hold my hand and to tell me that my Dad died. He had a massive heart attack at work that morning. He was gone, along with a huge piece of my heart, and it was way too much for me to handle. I buried my face in my hands and screamed all the way home. As I walked into the house there were so many relatives, friends, and all of my siblings, and there wasn't a dry eye to be seen. Everyone was so upset and it was completely overwhelming. I was numb inside and cried myself to sleep every night for a year. I didn't miss a night, not one. I told myself that he was on a business trip and he'd be home soon. I was grasping at anything to try and mask the pain. I was in total denial and wanted to return to school as soon as possible. I needed something to be normal to help me forget the nightmare I was in. I truly have no words for that loss and the feelings of abandonment. My stomach pain never seemed to go away. The void and aching in my heart was unbearable. I missed him so much! This was the start of many painful and depressing years. I never knew so many tears could be shed, but what I did know was that my life as I knew it was over.

The enemy grabbed hold of me tight and took away all of my daydreams and turned them into nightmares. My battle with depression, anxiety, and unhealthy thoughts began, and continued spiraling out of control for many years. I started Therapy since that's what I was told I needed but I was sent to Group Therapy. It was actually perfect because I wouldn't talk about my own problems, instead I'd try to help others with theirs, sharing compassion and keeping the focus off of my deep rooted pain. Hiding behind my fake smile and sarcasm, I barely made it through Junior High. I didn't know anyone who had lost their Dad suddenly and so I suppressed everything. The pain was never ending.

At sixteen I started working in an office as a Secretary and was being sexually and verbally harassed daily. I had no confidence and was broken down and led to believe that I had no worth. I was constantly being told that no one would ever hire me because of my lack of intelligence. I believed it all and stayed for 4 years. High School was a new journey of emotions. Dealing with my job was stressful and degrading but I hid it well. I met a great guy and was in an interracial relationship. He was funny and loved sports and dancing like I did. He was a football player and I was a softball player, and a cheerleader. I managed to keep a C average because participating in the games and cheering for them is what kept me going to school. We both enjoyed playing sports and going to each other's games. High School seemed safe inside those halls and walls. I could handle the scowls, fake smiles, and being excluded because I had mastered masking my pain in public. Outside of those walls, it was so much worse. I was spit on, glared at in disgust, laughed at, or just blatantly ignored. I was called many names not worth repeating. One time we had huge rocks thrown at us across a busy street. As they landed, missing us by inches, those good throwing arms were wasted on people whose mouths were screaming nonsense and obscenities. He never showed his pain and would remind me not to worry about what people say or think. Our eyes were wide open and our silence was the safest way to navigate through it. I had a glimpse of the harsh reality that not everyone really does Love thy Neighbor. It was hard to understand because racism didn't exist in my mind and never will!

I remember when I called him to tell him that I met the man I was going to marry, and he said "I know you went through World War III for me and I wish you nothing but the best." I told him it was worth every moment and that I would always treasure him, his family, and the good times we had shared together.

You never know where God is leading you. As fate would have it He had me visit a friend in Westwood one evening on my way home from work. Interestingly enough it was not my regular workplace but was the main office in the city. I was only working there for a week because I had reported my boss to Human Resources for discrimination and harassment. During my annual review she did not focus on my work performance but instead shared with me that I shouldn't let any of the higher-ups know that I had been in an interracial relationship. She had seen me at our company picnic when I bumped into my ex-boyfriend and we talked, exchanged a hug, and he went back to playing basketball. She took that moment in time and all of the work I had done that year was negated. I sat staring at her in astonishment and asked what she thought of the job I was doing. She rattled off some nonsense and I marched out of there and made the call to HR. I spent a week in the main office and she had found another place of employment. So, I did stop by to see my friend and had a drink and chat with her. After our short visit I headed out the door and a guy was walking in and our eyes met. It was Love at first sight when I saw him. My heart was pounding and I couldn't stop staring at him, so I turned around and went right back in. I headed over to the bartender and nervously fixed his tie and made small talk. My friend came over and I told her why I had about-faced and was at the bar again. As the guy found a chair, he positioned himself so he could look at me. I'd glance over but was well aware of the company he was with and didn't want to make a scene. I put my number on a matchbook and left it with the bartender. I told him that guy seemed interested and if he asked, he could give him the matchbook. How I had the courage to do that is still beyond me. I left again without him noticing and he called me the next day. Our Love was undeniable and God had orchestrated our divine appointment.

I thought I could leave all of my worries and cares behind but depression has a way of hiding, and then rearing its ugly head at the most inopportune times. Therapy was absolutely essential in my late twenties. I found it helped a tremendous amount to sit one-on-one and cry for an hour trying to work through the gut-wrenching pain of losing my Dad. Suppressing pain takes a toll on your body and mind. There were other traumas that needed to be brought to light and finally dealt with as well.

As time went on, we started a family and have 3 wonderful children. We decided that I would become a stay-at-home Mom and it was quite an adjustment both emotionally and financially. I remember going to a Pawn Shop to sell all of my gold to buy groceries. I only received $80.00 for the most exquisite jewelry, but we needed food on the table. I had not begun my Journey with Jesus when my kids were young. I spent years yelling at them and not handling stress well at all. I drank as much wine as I could, thinking I'd party like I did, well that didn't work. Drinking and drugs have a way of temporarily masking our pain and grief, only to wake up the next morning to try and deal with life. I became friends with other Moms who also liked to party and all was well until my anger would get the best of me the day after a Girls Night out. The hamster wheel was spinning and I was running on it full speed ahead and going nowhere fast. God sees all and knew that I needed Him to reach down and grab a hold of my heart, and take me off that wheel freeing me from the vicious cycle. As it turns out, one of the Moms introduced me to a Man of God. He prayed with me and Jesus remembered who I was, He saw where I had been, He saw that I was lost, He met me right where I was at, and He forgave me, but it was years before I would forgive myself.

I started the Journey with Jesus and attended a church and was baptized and began the work I needed to become who He wanted me to be. It wasn't always easy to look in the mirror and reflect on some of the things I had done. The enemy likes us to tread in the cesspool of guilt and shame to keep us stuck in our in our old ways and ungodly thoughts. There came a time in our life when we got behind in our house payments and it went into foreclosure. The stress was overwhelming along with the correspondence from the bank and overnight mail that seemed to arrive almost daily. Fortunately my husband kept his head about him and thankfully his Uncle helped with deciphering it. I on the other hand, found myself curled up in a ball, praying and losing sight of Jesus. It was during that storm that He would get me up in the middle of the night and put words on my heart to transfer to paper. The Lord was all I had and He got my attention and got me up to give me His words. Sadly I hid them under my bed, never thinking or believing He would want me to share them. Why would He choose me, a Sinner, but He did and I am so Humbled and Forever Grateful! What the devil means for harm, God will turn around for good!

I remember I used to drive to the church I grew up attending and sit in the parking lot and cry. My cries were not heard outside of my car and the light of the moon was my view through my tears. I never felt worthy enough to go inside during the day for a Sunday Service. The enemy had filled me with so much guilt and shame that it always overshadowed my worth. There are layers to our lives that are peeled away as we walk through the fires and in Faith. While we shouldn't look back on our plow, there are times when our reflections can't be denied, and we recognize the Deep Gratitude of being pulled out of the trenches and into His Loving and Forgiving arms.

For the past 10 years I have had the pleasure of working with students in elementary school. I'm happy to help anyone with focusing and comprehension because I understand it all too well. I try to encourage kids to use their imagination during playtime, and I also like to deal with "problem resolution" (arguments) on the yard, which leads to apologies, and then forgiveness. I feel it is important for them to learn to take responsibility for their actions, learn to apologize, (make eye contact and say sorry like you mean it) forgive, and move on. Learning Kindness and Forgiveness pays off and makes for fun days on the playground. I am Grateful that God opened the door and placed me where He saw that I am needed most. I am also happy that my current job is a safe place and I'm no longer being harassed.

I am so Grateful for my sister and my children who have supported me on my journey. I am Grateful for my Husband who has been by my side through all of it, and has found his way to The Lord as well. Our eyes met for a reason and our Love has endured many storms. This journey, our Family, and his Love and Support has shown me how Faithful and how Good God truly is!

I miss my Dad and I pray I've made him proud. I have Peace in knowing that he is with Jesus, whole and healed, with the best seats in the house for any sporting event. He Appreciated Athletes and their God-Given talents and he taught me to do the same no matter what team they played on. I was told he was an excellent athlete when he was young, but never by him. My Dad was very humble and he always said that people are more impressed with your abilities if you don't talk about them. He thought it was best to surprise them with your talent because you never live up to your boastings.

Again, my Hope is that something on these pages touches your heart, heals your heart, and inspires you to take time for yourself and write what He shares with you. I Hope you're inspired to pray for others and to be kind to people who cross your path from all walks of life; you never know what they are hiding behind their smile or sarcasm. Remember to always Give God the Glory knowing that You are His, You are Chosen, and You are Worthy! He is still on The Throne and He has a Plan for You! Pray, Spread His Love, Believe, and Receive!

✝

"And He said unto me, My grace is sufficient for thee: for My strength is made perfect in weakness. Most gladly therefore will I rather glory in my infirmities, that the power of Christ may rest upon me."
2 Corinthians 2:9

"Be merciful unto me, O God, be merciful unto me: for my soul trusteth in thee: yea, in the shadow of thy wings will I make my refuge, until these calamities be overpast. I will cry unto God most high; unto God that performeth all things for me. He shall send from heaven, and save me from the reproach of him that would swallow me up. Selah. God shall send forth his mercy and his truth."

Psalms 57:1-3

In Loving Memory
of my Mom …

IN LOVING
MEMORY OF MY MOM

———⟨∼⟩———

I n the interim of waiting to publish my book, I lost my Mom to Covid. Prior to her passing she was hospitalized but was released by the Grace of God and returned to her assisted living facility for Hospice Care. We were then able to go to her window and cry, pray, play music, and say our painful goodbyes. She was located on the bottom floor which made it accessible. Due to the many restrictions from Covid, we weren't allowed inside even though she was no longer contagious. I asked one of the Nurses if she would allow me in so I could hold her hand and take a picture. She said yes but only when the others left. I treasure that moment and picture so much. (A suggestion from a dear friend) It had been a year since we had hugged and held hands. I quickly left and went back to the window to play music, cry, and pray. Across the globe we all experienced the same pain from the isolation and lack of human contact during the pandemic.

I spoke to my Niece who lives out of state and she said she'd want to be in that room and not want to leave. She would call so I could hold the phone next to her ear since we were told that hearing was the last to go. I did it for others so they could get their goodbyes in too. On day 3, I took my Nieces advice and spent hours in my Mom's room. I brushed her hair and put some cream on her skin, played some of her favorite songs, and told her how much I loved her. I am so Grateful for my time with her. The painful days of saying goodbye, praying, playing music, and the never-ending tears left an indelible mark on my heart. Mourning while someone is still alive is a journey that only Jesus can carry us through. We did not have the gift of time to say goodbye when my Father suddenly passed away. The abrupt ending and unspoken words get stored away and can come out through tears at any given time.

It was such a Blessing that we had the time to say goodbye to my Mom. I thought about what it would be like to be with her when she was called to go home. Everyone talks about that sacred moment. My sister got a call from the Hospice Nurse that Mom had started to have labored breathing. The clock had just passed midnight and she texted us all with the news. My sister called me and we decided to head over. We were both only 10 minutes away, so I quickly got out of my pajamas and got layered up. I prayed in the car in what seemed like a half hour drive. As I arrived in the parking lot I saw my sister on her phone, and I knew we didn't make it in time. I walked up and she told me that she was gone. My other Sister arrived and we all hugged and cried. I so wanted to be in there to hold her hand for her last breath, but that wasn't God's Divine plan. The Nurse later shared with my sister that she saw the figure of a man enter her room right before she passed away. We are all convinced it was our Dad who had patiently waited forty two years to hold her hand again, so he could escort her to meet Jesus. If we would have been in the room, that beautiful story could not be told.

I decided to include "What I Learned from My Mom." I read it aloud at her Celebration of Life and was able to suppress my tears after I read the first few sentences. I consider it a Divine Delay to be able to add a dedication to my Mom also. Once again God showed me that His timing is perfect. We never want to say goodbye, but knowing where she is, and who she's with, gives me Peace.

"We are confident, I say, and willing rather to be absent from the body, and to be present with the Lord."

2 Corinthians 5:8

"To every thing there is a season, and a time to every purpose under the heaven: A time to be born, and a time to die; a time to plant, and a time to pluck up that which is planted; A time to kill and a time to heal; a time to break down, and a time to build up; A time to weep, and a time to laugh; a time to mourn and a time to dance; A time to cast away stones, and a time to gather stones together; a time to embrace, and a time to refrain from embracing; A time to get, and a time to lose; a time to keep, and a time to cast away; A time to rend, and a time to sew; a time to keep silence, and a time to speak; A time to love, and a time to hate; a time of war, and a time of peace."

Ecclesiastes 3:1-8

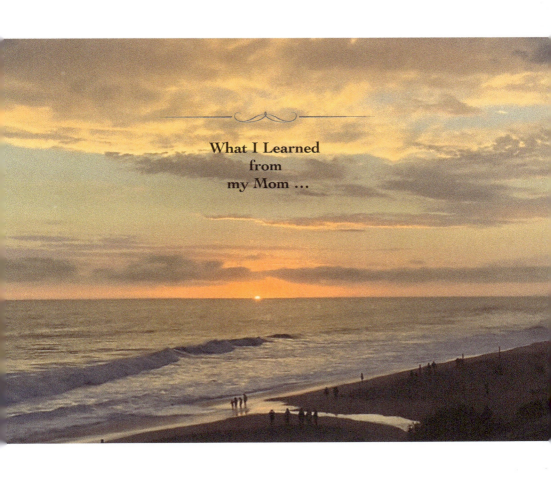

What I Learned
from
my Mom …

I learned to never miss an opportunity to teach your children, even in the car, the ABC game, States and Capitol game, reading signs, and who could read it first…

I learned to be productive while watching television…

I learned it took a week to pack for a trip no matter how long the trip was…

I learned that a polyester mixed suit doesn't wrinkle, and it's a great outfit to wear on a plane… (not that I ever did)

I learned how to iron…

I learned not to wear white in winter… (but I was a rebel and did it anyway)

I learned that your clothes should match and that you always knew what was "all the rage"…

I learned to never look back …

I learned to never give up…

I learned to be fair even though life isn't…

I learned how to plan for dinner in the morning…

I learned to decorate…

I learned to use doilies in cookie tins between the layers and on cake platters…

I learned how to clean with TSP…

I learned the best way to ruin a party is to talk about Politics or Religion…

I learned that you can't leave a chocolate shaving behind on the kitchen counter or you'll get nailed for eating the frozen See's egg stash …

I learned how important it is to eat a meal with someone…

I learned that Fruit Cocktail was considered a treat… (and I'm still not sure why)

I learned it is much easier to accept your circumstances than to complain about them…

I learned that a smile can brighten someone's day…

I learned to talk to the checkers at the grocery store and let them know how much they are appreciated…

I learned to treat Everyone with Respect…

I learned how good it feels to give…

I learned how to read a map…

I learned to appreciate old movies …

I learned to appreciate Tap Dancing...

I learned to enjoy the sentimental value...

I learned the Twinkie's in the freezer were all accounted for...

I learned to never arrive empty handed...

I learned how to play cards...

I learned to be competitive ~ and if you don't win the first game, you play the best out of 3...

I learned to root for the underdog...

I learned to clean under my bed before company came over... although I still don't know why...

I learned to welcome new neighbors into the neighborhood and bake them cookies...

I learned that if you saute' onions and garlic it makes the house smell really good...

I learned that music is a mood changer...

I learned to enjoy the dance floor...

I learned to listen and appreciate the stories being told at the dinner table...

I learned that you can laugh at the same joke or story just as hard, even if you've heard it more than 10 times...

I learned to laugh at myself first...

I learned that laughter is contagious...

I learned to be humble…

I learned to look on the bright side…

I learned to answer to Trace, Bri, Ker…

I learned how to paint…

I learned to Appreciate Art…

I learned to never make fun of people…

I learned to join committees and try to make a difference…

I learned to pay attention to the details…

I learned the joy of cooking and entertaining…

I learned to wear an apron…

I learned to go the extra mile…

I learned that Kindness has no limits…

I learned how to hide my liver and onions in my salad…

I learned to do the border of a puzzle first…

I learned to appreciate traveling… you were so excited we were going to Paris and wanted us to take the kids to Italy, one day…

I learned that you can freeze anything (just label it and date it)…

I learned how strong you were and to keep moving forward…

I learned that you going back to college at 50 to get your Art degree was everything … and you never stopped encouraging me to do the same…

I learned about the power of prayer and having Faith in God!

I learned how much you loved your Mom and how much you missed her, especially during the Holidays. From today on I will miss you too! I Love You and I Thank You for teaching me all of these things and much more!

As you used to say to me "I Love You, Love You, Love You, God Bless" and right back at you Mom! Enjoy your time with Dad, your Family, your Friends, and especially with Jesus! With so much Love and Appreciation for You, Kerry XOXO

"The Lord bless thee, and keep thee: The Lord make his face shine upon thee, and be gracious unto thee: The Lord lift up his countenance upon thee, and give thee peace."
Numbers 6:24-26

"He that dwelleth in the secret place of the most High shall abide under the shadow of the Almighty. I will say of the Lord, He is my refuge and my fortress: my God; in him will I trust."
Psalms 91:1 & 2

CPSIA information can be obtained
at www.ICGtesting.com
Printed in the USA
LVHW072125061121
702640LV00018B/135